A Thousand Windows

A Thousand Windows

A Book of Poetry

Coy Williams

A Thousand Windows
Coy Williams / Napa, California
www.CoyWilliamsPoetry.com

Printed in the United States of America.

ISBN: 978-0-9893081-3-7

Library of Congress Control Number: 2013942022

POETICUS®
PUBLISHING
www.PoeticusPublishing.com

For

Ephraim Sando

"Come dance through me
in this ancient body
aligned with the stars wheeling.

Day will fall into night
and your pain and shadows
will fill my empty glass
and I will drink your darkness
with the light.

And a thousand wings
will blush the pillars of rose
within an ocean of polar eyes.

And the blood will thunder
through the great heart
and the tiny fingers
will reach over the arctic sun
to touch the hand
dreaming of warmer birds."

CONTENTS

I

II

III

IV

THE YEAR

I

Hearts of Water

Sometimes,
in this deep falling,
I think of you.

You are the river song
singing lovers invisible,
consuming and drowning,
traveling through each other.

From the red rocks singing
dried orchards of stone
where hiding red lions vanished
and desert gorges lay bleeding earth.

Hand in hand the memories from each pool clears,
a thought of you, a shadow darting from the rocks.

Hearts of water rushing to fill,
the bells turning
to gold.

Wild Lily

Remember the dark silent glove?

You slipped the layered, silent earth—
came up the long walk,
up through the white mist.

I remember the love
immortal and wild,
soaked in rain.

We weaved petals web, drawn in,
searched the air,
the thirsty touch.

Tears came,
feeling life spring fire
burning time in the sun.

Summer innocence,
weeping stem-white
over the fields.

Lonely at times for understanding,
I look for you
in the dark leaves,
holding out your hands.

Spring

The night clings to her drifting hair,
climbs into furrows of gold
where he once taught her eyes to see.

The seasons are clouds
swept into the day
changing songs
of brackish breath.

Lands under the earth
warming, rotting,
laughing spring.

Radiant green leaves
with cupped hearts in love.
Golden ships on fire
lay sail in bloom
taking her away.

The hungry frenzy
of blind spring
will give life to anyone.
Corrupt, dark purpose to anyone;
Imposing trees,
grass or flowers pretense;

weeps and laughs,
grows and learns how to sing.

Coming Home

Make me a place
beneath the field
where the grass is tall and golden.

Let me soar
when the rotting turns to air
this child of fire.

Show me the brook
where the Red-winged blackbird sings.

Lay your breath on my cheek
one last time.
Kiss the ache from my long journey.

Your love will carry me through
the great mouth,
where the torrents and dark
become light.

Lead me across the meadows
to the seas' black glass.

Open the door
if it will not open.
Hold my hand
so I will not be afraid.

Sing the song I longed to hear,
open my eyes
so I can see.

Mirror

Where have you gone—
The seconds, hours and days
endless running water
between long winters snow
and summer grass?

Your youth has gone
slipping away from the child
on a swing.
Push me! Higher! Higher!
Until the chains
became loose as air.

Leaves fall on the window,
secrets are playing half open
wandering in the night
still a child.

I dream
When I held you,
the mask in the water stood still
and the moon of your lips
was open and full.

And that day became a year
and a lifetime of seasons
old and beautiful
as your face.

Tin Man

There are shadows
long turning pins,
belonging to silent keys
each with its own secret shape
unlocking in the motion of the afternoon sun.

And the door opens from the west.
And somewhere the desert rain
paints the fountain copper,
bleeding rocks
whispering.

Listen to the time
rushing by.
It is the silence
of rust.
It is the heart
of the tin man.

Longing For Spring

Above the moon
lifting over ground the smell of night.

Where tigers walk on clouds
above the rain soaked gardens
in earth's upper sky.

Waltzing across the breath,
bodies of women
wrapped tight around me
and slept there.

Below, the antique lace veil
lifts across the music,
of wind and glass.

The water shines in the dark.
I hunger for your mouth
with the same desire,
divided by rain and night—
currents across the earth.

I plan to find you
in the garden dirt
if not in the water or the rose,
I will look in the air for your body
or the stars filled with light.

Time in Variation

Down through the tiers, long amble climb—
the boy dipped his shirt in a spring
and wiped his eyes.

The wood's hidden ponds
appear as black snakes
crawling in the leaves;

And beneath the cliff,
hands of yellow fern
wave him in.

In this dark sanctuary
of mid summer,
a boy might choose to swim naked,
unnoticed by the clouds that pass above
or a girl miles away.

Even be forgotten completely by death,
or the constant rhythm of his breath,
or maybe be forgiven, for things not yet done—
for things men must,
or must not do.

Holding his breath in the pond—
submerged for a time
in variation.

Daylight

The moon rose triumphant,
a blind, brilliant ghost
whispering of centuries.

Ribbons wrap the seeds
of white cities in the sky.
And the crown the fog has made you,
crazy premonition over the heart,
lifts and falls
passing to the south.

The moonlight streaks the yard,
the beasts stand still.

The trees call to the shore
and the night goes out with the tide
as the waves fall into the sea.

The wind touches your face,
late and long as your lover sleeps
and signals the hour before it comes;
to hold the door
the discerning eyes,
before the fearless child, awakes.

Willow Bark

Walking out on the waters edge
pointing to the country burning
in the evening sky.
We lay down in pink mirrors
of summer.

In the sky over head
two hands of water and light
press together
casting red ashes
over the dark sea,
where berries shadow
blue swarms of light.

The waves are warm across our breath
and the air is mixed
with willow bark.

Summer Fountain

There are fields in the sky
where women's eyes are summer,
and light blue water
fingers the clouds to shape.

I search the cheek
on the hills,
and run the shadows of brooks
through the woods.

I feel on my skin
the cool petals of your breath
that lift and fall from your sparkling eyes.

And I whisper in the flow
of your hair
for your smile and lips
to drown me.

Rising Moon

Rising moon
of a thousand faces
and my heart an island of sand.

Nobody but you
in a moment
could stop me,
your lips of silver and dark.

The thirst always calls me
back to the night,
back into your arms
until my eyes
are full of wings.

Night Bird

I hear in the wind
low breathing calling me to the sea.

From these petals' open lips,
I soar in the night sky
on the endless mouth of surf,
crying echoes above the waves.

I cut the slits of air and voice,
flip over darting the light.
Speeding towards the moon,
running from the shadows of wolves,
on the glass below.

Effortless, these pastures,
as I dance across the dark cathedral
of night.

Moth

When the weight of dreaming
has taken you—
Two lovers
hold the golden lamp.

Opening through the darkness
a white moth dreams
mysterious circles,
and the spinning light
becomes bodies, opening and closing.

From flesh to wind
the flame is emerald,
and the tiny eyes tremble
closing once, twice,
then flashes to smoke.

Earthworks

There are voices rotting leaves
with timeless care;
seasoned stacked,
murmuring dark purpose.

Inside you where the sound is deafening,
deep decay falls off burning silence.
My hungry root penetrates your moist sod.
The fingers go deep,
careful not to disturb your winter's late friend.

Below the skin our tapestry blooms.
I take your essence without a word;
Clutching white stones and amber,
you lean back.
Our bodies soaked
the corridor of laughter,
white stems reaching the touch.

Hungry mouth open,
the dark planet sifts through the last storm.
The spine heaves the roof's canopy
calling currents, running deep.

Holding on to one another
we curl beneath the long white pitch.
Gripping the rail
our fingers hold tight to the ice,
the snow's white breath to break,
feeling blind
for the coast of spring.

Evergreen

Relentless is my song
that never stops.
It grows outward
as a shadow of a bird,
silent as a woman's hair
wanting to be touched.

I miss you in these days,
when the gray veil of longing
stretches on the road
with rain,
and curls the night
with waves of music,
lifting and falling.

I dream
invisible currents,
like heaven eclipsed by birds,
their song
cutting through skies' eternity,
evergreen.

Rain

Laughing bells
ring out your voice from heaven.
Cut loose from your full, gray fields.
Roll to the last strand of thunder,
your dark eyed desire.
Shake your head and let it fall.

Your beauty is water;
the language of the river's wide snake,
subtle black eel of the brook,
the pond's belly cupped mirror
and the sea's vast, naked back.

You sing through the babble
and clatter of the rocks,
and tease in the lifting waves
where the doves curl in foam at your mouth,
then disappear.

I am the earth you arouse.
You rub against me soft tickling
and I respond,
stirring life, milky stream pale.

And the petals of my soul break free
quivering skyward in the sun
for your cheek.

And I laugh clear my freedom over earth,
clear blue of sky and breath
in the dominion of your lips.

Song of the Tide

Swirling,
her cape romantic.
Winds of white music,
spray the air with doves.

Upward pockets of cold and warm,
streak the night in northern lights,
across a galactic spine.

Between each other they nod,
to the same direction,
those herds of moving gray
that come for miles undaunted,
all blind, gentle beasts
pulled to their careless bay.

Lifting her eyes inland,
she moves deep and wanting.
Her solvent womb holds a red hunger.
Her vivacious, bloom lifts the throbbing swell,
to plunge and crawl the soft sod.

She licks her teeth
within the broken rocks,
her breath low, rising to foam,
breaks the open air,
pulled deep to scrape the sandy lust,
that rolls off shoulders
of smooth stones,
against the relentless sleep.

Bone Fish

The sun burns the blue oracle,
tracing the sky in a boundless sea.

It is endless this constant ringing bell,
melodic voice through metal
holding my body.

Between the dull curve and stone face,
I search the gardens'
sentient flowers.

The white violin weeps
and the voice heats the water
through my body.

It is the steel hook
that pulls me
as thunder sweats the cord
from silence.

White Heron

Where does it go,
The soul's white heart;
the moon's petals
falling on black glass?

With the tide's endless pull,
oblivion floats white
bobbing and turning
music to wind.

What has brought you
to this outlet,
stalking the weeds,
icy spear, burning hot?

Yours is not the dream of water
or the stars mouth open.
It is not a flame
that draws your face
to the pool.

Your moon hovers
for more then a breath,

it stares down for me.

Raven

I ride the edge from wolves and twilight.
Dark cavern, ravenous death,
dwells the flying thief
stealing golden crumbs.

I am drawn to him,
neither master or friend,
I hold out my hand anyway.
My broken bread of dreams
I will share.

Come here!
Tell me what is behind your dark eyes
and why you hunger so,
for my last breath.
Why do you wait so calmly for me,
cutting the soft throat of day
with your cry?

Can you tell me if hell has teeth,
and heaven but temperate lips?
And might I hear angels
as I pass down your throat's
black dominion,
to silence.

The Loon

The voice of the loon is in me.
It feathers within my bed
all memory of you.

Ancient love calling,
spirit of the night,
who will return your call?

Has night forgotten you?
Will day sweep the voices clear
and fold its wings around you?

Will the chanting shore die
without your silver ribbons
torn in the night sky?

Will I always remember,
when your shrouded call
opened the blackness,
searching the night at the same spot,
the same darkness of this earth
alone?

Can I taste the notes in your mouth?
Can I ever live without its call?

Kisses from the Dead

So many nights
I spoke your name
as you slept.

Hearing you breathing
next to me,
with the sound of a cricket
outside the window.

I asked, why am I here?
The cricket answered for you.

Love asleep,
under the blue road,
on silver rivers of dust.

Beneath your eyelids
a different name
sleeps with you.

Rainbow beneath the mountain,
kisses from the dead.

Two Hearts

Away from you,
the day has two hearts.
One with desire of your mouth and body
which beats with fire,
the other beats softer, coming sweet,
like a child's love wrapped around my neck.

Images of your body flash through the day
over streets and objects without form,
appearing like swallows darting past.
And my blood is hot from it,
and it takes over like rain.

Then softly,
the tears of your life come to view,
like snow and music
and I am helpless but to love you.

And I hold you as an ancient love
both father and mother and words.
All in one desire to reach the pain,
to stroke your hair
until your heart runs clear
with room to love me.

To fall together in that grasp
of spirit and sky.
Where our bodies take over
both animal and breath.

And when we meet later on
our words are but shields
from the thoughts of the day,
looking for the door to open
the sky again.

Candle Smoke

I remember when you came into my life.
Barely a whisper, wind at the door.
Across the room gliding with ease,
a swallow carrying ribbons of light.

And I wanted you
in that moment, like a flower.
To hold beauty,
to claim for myself, your sweetness.

I never imagined out of such a look
my desire would grow.
To what end my love would go weeping
in the harvest of your heart.
And in your arms
the language would be molded,
flamed in passion.

We were one form,
a wick muddled fate,
burning itself without end.

And the spirit in which we burned
lit the night beyond all words,
the air filled
eternity.

II

Untitled

And I wished to die,
not knowing you would leave me—

And the sons and daughters of the leaves,
would fall in the autumn
and the blood between words and life
would go on,
past the winter fear
reaching a pure absolute place,
swirling strips of gold
that never touch the ground.

Her Dream Was the Universe

In the sand
beneath the shifting, dark mantle,
layers dream the summer's rain
stacked one by one over voice.

Once
roses epiphany
arbored the great columns' thigh,
calling into the flames.

She knew in the stars
when the dark magnificent
would leak out
upon the ground.

And in time
I would come to rub away the veil,
covering her lips.

The sun of her passion still burns
the cheek within the ashes.
Her wind moving over syllables
speak of roses
and kisses.

My hands
sift the still breath
between sand and desire,
in a land I have never been.

Beneath her body burns
a garden of tears
flooding the chamber with horses,
running ribbons around
lovers and kings

The Dust Storm

An eloquent whisper,
the trembling bird escapes
as in the distance
gray clouds stir the ground.

You stood at the edge of an island
in silence, holding still in a turning world,
as a dust storm rolled towards you
pulling sand and thunder.

What brought you to this place
in witness of your own need?
Your incidental soul
fixed as a star.

Feeling small you cried for help,
and across a million nights,
a sound tied with white ribbons
curling the air of cities,
came to me.

And I found your hand reaching
and never let it go.

The Key

I put your body
on the face of smooth stones,
and those stones on the face of stars.
I rub the day below the belly
as my footsteps fill with ashes.

The absence is deafening still.
A wounded animal cries
between thoughts
and silence.

A symphony plays,
harbors the slate gray lock
its rusted face weeping.

When I was with you,
both innocence and fire
burned the fields red.
Now from this door
the night holds its hand
over my eyes.

Alone,
in a turn beneath this heart,
the vast plain opens
where we hid as children
within the grass, stealing passion,
dreaming the sky of clouds.

I was only a dream.
And you were only poetry.

It Always Happens

Every time you leave me,
there is an absence I cannot explain.
Like the wind stopping on an open sea,
or hearing your voice in the other room,
long after you have gone.

It speaks from the silent leaves of roses.
It soars in the clouds overhead.
It is elusive,
like water over stones.

Like a child I turn
from your arms,
to the flutter of daybreak
as your kiss leaves the morning
without a trace.

I am jealous at life
taking you,
even for a moment.

And I laugh at my desire
and foolish heart to think,
the ruffled sheets on the alter you left me,
could keep me safe
from loving you.

Because Of You

Pressed against me
arms connected,
your soft burning voice
is an endless river that glistens
on golden river streams,
of thoughts washed and tumbled.

I love you
as my heart opens and closes,
empties and fills.

I have peered out this window before
on life's changing face.
Eyes in a photograph I can't recall.
Untouchable secrets as a boy
in beautiful, lazy summers.

I close the curtain
as sunlight feeds the small man
standing near the fence.
And he is staring up at me as a red rose.
And I am veiled with planets spinning,
my breath born in the blinding light.

Only God can see through me
singing the years invisible,
before I knew life,
before I would come to life,
because of you.

Bell

Take my heart
endless calling out.

Breathe in my broken voice
lifting tender
over the hills.

It is not of any shape
this rusting metal frame.

It is a bell
splitting
the air sharp
doorway.

Morning

Waking,
her long hair
lifts half-hearted shadows
over the fields.

The light flickers in her eyes,
her cheeks blush the morning
that steps over stones
in white camellia.

Cautious,
her enormous heart
spreads out clouds like leaves,
looking for her lover.

Eloquent the whisper
lifting slowly,
her light searches the faces
in windows and doorways.

Sweet, invisible presence
once again
imagining herself.

Spring Song

From winter
I listen for your voice
in the silent moon.

I try not to remember
the flower of your passion,
the feel of your body
haunting me over smooth shoulders of fog,
your soft breath pulling me in the night.

I breathe trembling water,
a thousand sparrows flickering
in my lips.

Hovering over your fields,
the wings beat in my chest
gurgling the racing waters
down brooks of melting snow.

Up from your damp sod,
your sea continues to swell
as your hair of sunlight
sweeps across my chest.

Sweet spring of desire,
calling my name
beneath the earth.

Lupines

I looked out across the field
and saw lupines growing
in the spring morning.

I spoke to them—
Give me more, a sweet sound;
subtle, lifting the ladle,
pouring smoothly out.

Teach me the day
with two voices—
thirst and light.

Just enough
to clear my throat
of yesterday.

Shallow is the dust
and water that touches us.

Might I imagine
we are all born without words—

Only eyes
and spirit.

Vespers

Woman of my thirst—
infinite longing.

The night holds you in a sign
burning for me,
ancient symbols of a prayer.

Scattered eyes pull me in,
one to the next.
Petals flickering, a thousand breaths.

I am yours, listening for voices
over riverbeds
crying water on a distant moon.

From this garden hungry to know you,
to make some connection,
your mouth opens between points on a map
that speak beyond the dark expanse
of lovers arching in the nights blackness.

First Thaw

Winter
in its broken,
long cold air
surrender—

Disbelieving blue sky
with anxious birds,
wake mountains sleeping in snow
with bristled backs—

Awaken thirsty caverns
with crystal lashes
crying nonstop.

Moonlight embers
cascade down melting ice;
speeding, earth bound heartbeats
with shameless pretensions
of a broken wing.

Spring Symphony

My breath is the night
your arms the seductive sun.

Let these petals fall
from your rose.

Let your snow covered hills, uncover
and the pine limbs direct.

Let the starlings mark the sky
in black swirling smoke.

Let the cold moon's face
unveil its softer light.

Let the bell beneath the sea
ring out the shells.

Let these hands cup your breasts of earth
and my mouth consume your sweet,
fragrant lips of spring.

Above

Forgive me for remembering,
a child often needs to feel
what it was like to hold miracles
in his hands.

I hold on now for the sun,
around me the smell of dreams
and roses decay.

Over dark waters,
I hold on to my soul like smoke
lingering from ancient candles.

Deep in my chest
birds migrate crying
for the last summer's breath
when I loved you,

when in the night
a necklace of stars
fell from your neck
and I wished I could fly
above the rain and currents,

and never feel the cold air
without you.

Night Books

In a paragraph of her lips,
the words are seeds
open to fly,
tasting each other
like dirt and rain.

The salt is a naked shadow
of a woman's deep and endless desire,
holy water to bathe his face.

And the mask that he wears
is only leaves falling,
and the thief of the moon is a poem,
pages of white echoes
from the heart,
that lift and turn to doves
in her hands.

Waiting For the Leaves

On Tuesday the dream came again,
burning in the night.

We would push the deep grass aside
and lay down—
racing hearts in flames.

All the land turned to desire,
anytime, anywhere we burned.

And the longing grew
deep in those fields, new and open.

And I loved you like the sun
making patterns on your body,
and the desert of my heart was alive.

Now without you,
I am haunted by those frozen images,
and the shadow of your voice
saying my name across my lifetime.

In my heart forever,
waiting for the leaves.

Starlight

When evening falls to the shadows,
I travel the dark side of the world.

The cusp of the womb is starlight,
It is you.
Moon or dark faced earth,
It is all you.

As I sleep with the night,
your skin is the darkness I touch.

Reaching out to you,
there are wings in the bones of my hands
that fly to the heaven of your lips.

I love you as the star that is never seen,
a beacon that I know is there
hidden in the dark.

The Dream Came Again

The dream came again—
A breeze pressing the warm invisible
of your body.

Lying in the deep grass
burning passion to rest,
roaming clouds in the sky
become kisses that hold your face.

Returning across the night,
I drift in the smoke
from a thousand candles
of your love,
softly leading me home.

The Year He Left

From a thousand windows
they lived in flowers for her sake.
And the passion was in their faces,
and sunset laughed
a slim fading laugh.

And the voice of the roses
made her believe
they were all for her.

And I know her heart
will never give up
the search for him,
her body burning secrets.

There must be a place
across the dark rain
that she can last
the lies to herself as easily
as his gate down the long summer night.

Can the bones of her body
shake lose the absence?
Can the face in the moonlight
ever return his breath
to her cheek?

Girl down the Road

God
as a boy,
I tipped the scale
holding swallows
and little girls' dreams.

And the silent aura
of silken blades
cut the dreams
into night.

Your mending heart
had warm fire
that folded rivers
into amethyst.

My dream
still burns from those days
in mirrors of summer,
everlasting.

Girl down the road
who never knew
my heart
or how your memory
would soften
my destiny.

Promises

She thought of where the mind opened out
the safe falling of the words would save her
beneath the dark invisible, a place to hide.

Feeling the sculpture of his face,
brown sand and sea milk
in a cup full of promises
across her lips—

angels struggle to be free
as the glass breaks a thousand streams
of birds.

Resonance

It has been so long
since I heard your voice.

When I sleep,
faces and bodies
pass through layered thoughts of consciousness,
disappearing without color.

Life's insipid prose
has caught me like a river,
pulling me in a day to day
without sound.
Vacant rooms without light or darkness.

The longings are not the same.
My thoughts are one mixed sea of poetry.

I go to bed hungry
to hear your arms.

Tide Pools

Away from you,
life's frenzy lapped
its ivory tongue.
Moss on temple stones,
the arch over the bed.

A song without words
feels its way on the shore,
deep sea, red soundless.

Your body is the sky,
turning over burning sand.
Your hand searches for the child
among the sea shells,
a piece of driftwood,
a small heart beating.

Broken wings in your breast
that can not fly anymore,
long for love and stars

and the wings of children.

Before Time

Before time,
when the suns of galaxies
were threads of light
woven into your hair;

My fingers
of the night sky,
would softly feel for you,
in the grass and naked trees,
flying over the sea and breadth of rivers.

In the fragrant universe of night
within the silent pulse of stars,
where the shadows and soul
merge silver on your body,
flowing music like warm rain.

My fingers move up your leg
pulling stars across your skin.

And you squeeze my hand tight
and the small, silky curve of a fallen leaf
trembles without eyes,
leaving shadows of butterflies
in silver dust,
turning in the sky.

III

Reunion

Now, and all
timeless concord
flowed together
and made the night,
seeming resonant.

In throated signal
from whip-poor-will
it came calling.

Distant and slow
the old face appeared,
his dark overcoat
autumn shroud.

In call and dress
his presence kept
the dark woods there.

I called to him
to reach for atmosphere
out beyond the barn.

It sounded further out
past the woodpile
but I held from going further,
for I knew it then—
New England.

Picture Albums

Filtered light through Venetian blinds
bleeding through my fingers,
cutting the lines of my face,
a face forever passing through mirrors.

Pushing up these windows
glassless into the edge of the sky,
the sunlight flames the clouds
caught between doors of empty hallways.

I step down carpet-worn stairs
along silent, poorly lit corridors
to daylight and park bench wastelands.
From worn pockets, holding my dreams out
one by one, to pigeons
that fly away.

Returning to rented hours;
hands washed in years of weathered rain,
rest themselves
in armchairs and pale white stares.

Behind doors with teacup sighs and broken voices
in afternoon plays,
there, left breathing to the tick, of the clock
in white robes peeking out from behind the shades.

I can't turn away the stranger's face,
out windows, fading mirrors and absent looks,
from the tired worn beds unmade,
the foolish smiling child
sitting captive to dreams, escapeless,
in the afternoon of picture albums.

Ancients

I see glaciers in the light
and I hear swallows
gliding over the sea of glass, radiant.

Across centuries they moved,
in lands where the dark forests grew.
Where ancient women once gathered wood
for the fire to make bread.

And this world was bread,
consistent to the taste of blood,
the salt of the earth.

And I breathe their words
lingering in the air.
And I feel a presence
from that time,
from my father's father.

I long to live within their voices,
and resound their past in the frozen smoke.
I want to hear of the deer and the forests,
the horses and the rivers they broke
sounding hooves rushing over water.

I want to sing of the Great Spirit,
whose land it was and whose body
was the seed and tongue curled stream,
passing down the road's twilight.

Take me where the fogbow curling mist rises,
after the rain calls the sun.
Make me a necklace, proud earth,
of seeds and feathers, claws and teeth.
And give me strong arms of copper and longbow.

Speak softly from the name
carved in the white oak and hemlock,
beside the stream that still flows
in her eyes.

Speak now from the sentry
from the seasons watch,
with coat flowered woods with wings,
to the sky of warbled gray windows.

Red Spider

I don't know if the red spider
on the African plain will miss it.

Or in the wide sea,
if the whale's song
will show a change.

Will the white crane sensing it,
slow its step for me?

Will the orange dawn,
feather the field
one last time?
And snowcaps weep,
as I close my eyes?

Will the girls miss me,
in the summer grass?
Gathering wild kisses
in the sun.

Will autumn blackbirds, of swirling smoke,
feeling a loss within their pattern,
suddenly close formation?
Or will they leave a place of honor,
for me?

The earth is hungry just one more time
and the maples and the birches
fill the air with voice.

I will pass through the twilight
of the poets,
their eyes gleaming like stars.

They will sniff the dirt
and grass from my body
and search my pockets for leaves
and smooth stones.

The earth is hungry just one more time
and the maples and the birches fill the air.

Deer Hunter

When I was young in winter
in the woods of my home,
sleeping apples called out to the deer
and the sun would sound the warm opus,
rising cords of smoke.

Hunters of the fields,
my brother and I
searched for the deer
in haphazard wanderings,
following tracks through the woods,
and searched in the moonlight
for his face.

Apollo brother do you hear me?
I have blown the horn, calling you in the woods.
I have searched for you in the cedar grove
and in the rain for your voice.

Gone now with the silver body of snow,
bleeding water high above the ridge
where you went to wear the mask of the deer
and antlers my brother.

And in the alder swamps
and on the rubbing tree
you left your mark for me.

And I will remember
your tracks in the snow
and how I loved you
before I knew what love was.

My dear, ominous soul,
I will never forget
as I take your memory whole,
over my shoulders
through the alders
and out the blizzard's mouth.

The Conch

Breathless fog would come,
slicing the still invisible.
And a far off fog horn
will remind me,
of the waves of winter lions.

Heart in his neck,
the old horn could speak.
Beautiful, the old conch,
edges worn smooth,
black body that smelled of dirt.

The sound would echo in the woods
past the cliffs and Crocker farm,
the Griswold's and Wyatt's field.

It was a family sound
a signature of sorts,
that someone was in the woods.

It is my childish desire
that we all return as before.
Before life reshaped us,
hardened us
or took us.

When one voice was clear in its direction,
that old conch
leading us home.

One Small Hand

I didn't know you existed,
when leaves and night grew musty with fear.
When my body jerked in sleep,
running from lions,
tearing at my flesh, weeping.

I didn't know you existed,
when my dying brother cried
for your arm to hold on to.
When miles away his girlfriend closed a book,
blew out a candle, and went to sleep.

I didn't know you existed,
when madness, steel-eyed held my gaze,
crying fingers in melted wax,
waiting for the pain to stop.

I didn't know you existed,
when children held up their hands,
and cried for death
to make them laugh.

I didn't know you existed,
until night and day came close enough to sing,
in one voice,
one brother,
one small hand.

A Second Sky

When the waters of these days
cuts lines in your memory,
I piece together prayers
like old photographs.

The sweet heaven
that once filled my young life,
sweet heaven of your eyes
staring into mine.

I only hope,
the island that is your memory,
my words will not stumble,
will not fail you.

Steps must be gentle to remember
all the small things that you did.
To a child, the most important of all,
you taught me the sky,
and what clouds look like.

Now when I look into the clouds,
I look for you.

Never could I have imagined
in the grass that day,
the sweet heaven that filled my life,
sweet heaven of your eyes staring into mine,

could be so far away.

My Mother, in Heaven

You left behind
silver petals of ashes,
and a memory of your smile.

I can feel you,
your love is the stillness
the absence of everything,
the living of everything.

I know my words cannot be answered
but I feel an answer in the stars.
I know you are part of all that now
and again, all of nothing.

The open door that you traveled through
has closed behind you
and the brightness of its virtue,
only a vague shadow.

The elegance of the blue road
is clouded white with miles of prayers,
dipping and gathering into birds.

I know the answers
but find myself questioning everything
as if I was new to eternity,
bathed as a child singing in white temples,
the secret of being alone.

On Wednesday

The animals were quick
and fed leisurely on my body.
My skull seemed awkward now,
larger and out of place with the rest.
The bones laughed easy,
shining, scattered like a white rosary,
broken in the leaves of grass.

This is the land I finally see,
hidden desert in the growing grass,
vision upward to the open sky,
bound and free.
Free from the darkness beneath.
Free from inheritance,
rituals and plot.
Free of lilac in the dooryard blooming
and gathering voices from vacant lots.

No veiled woman's verse to soothe
or solid coffins laugh.
No pilot's hand to steer the bar
or face to face assume.
No miles to go, for woods or shore,
the autumn tide is still.
The odor of life has ended long,
the open sky has filled.

Time weaves the grass around me,
decay and tapestry.
I hold to every thread,
straining to see
where the two lines will cross
from twilight and horizon,
shroud to swaddling.

I peer out to the distant,
magnificent rib cage,
bleached like ivory gates.

Sweet One

Cobblestone England, the lords' descent.
Foot-locker journey
long to the place,
where the sunrise on the morning mast
and the orange glow,
touches on everything America.

I remember when dishes in the hutch
had shown the finest china
and the Irish filled the cups of guests
and the red rose that she wore
hooked deep its thorn in cameo white aster
against a blue sky.

I remember the harbor
in her frenzied midday spell,
where black sweat and burlap
mixed with the smell of the sea
and the moving sky rolled with the waves,
as captured faces searched the docks
with motherless eyes,
entranced, conclusion
in cane-sweet America, with ebony seeds.

And from the swelling calm and patient earth,
the cornucopia autumned
and the Indian summer
sweetly sang from her fields.

And the grapes that grew from the Promised Land,
clustered warm on the vine.
Through insipid summer
their passion grew,
bleeding joy for burning lips,
toast the wedding and sang.
Engaged the land, the dream together
yellow mustard, golden ring.

Within the iris, the rose, the grape's red heart,
into the song it all goes.
Into the seeds and voice, wilderness and desire,
into the singing blood.
Where the eyes cannot see
and dreams cannot yet vision, it all goes.
Through history's ringing steps,
into the soul's deep heart and out again.

The hand holds tight
this song of the earth,
the sweet ones, mothers bleed.
America's orb, the umbilical stem,
the child beyond the seed.

The Gathering

From the sweet breath of youth,
old grasses weave together in the wind.
Dreaming of seven brothers and four sisters,
suspended belief the wind could blow
out of trees, the wings of doves.

Old voices echo their steps,
white horses against a black mountain
running wild.

We traced the doves in the sky to the sea—
Went down, drowned in mirrors,
a thousand rings of dancing light in our eyes.
Our bare feet leaving tracks,
vanishing on the shore.

Together we bonded with mud,
our faces laughter—

As summer nights,
the Whip-poor-wills played
hide-and-seek with lightning bugs.

We gather now
to search for those pieces
that made us whole.

Pieces as easy in symmetry
as fallen stars.

IV

THE YEAR

January

Fountain's white branches
sparkle the air
in magnificent breath.

Climbing over the rocks of evening,
there is music in the fields of snow.

The wind is cold
but summer is warm in her heart.

She takes my hand and leads me
through the trees.

And the sun is darting on the road
that curves dreaming shadows
over the earthbound swells,
taking me to her side.

I breathe the fragrance of her there
and ask if we could be lovers.

She smiles
and speaks the only way she can,
offering her body
for an answer.

February

Bring to me
the taste of your lips on the rain,
as Spring comes fragrantly with your dress,
over the reef of the moon laid out.

And on your cheek, crystal voyage innocence,
plays the child of sleep.

Beautiful white web, roses along your walk,
temple green space between the snow.

The music of your body is soft fire
and the white fog along your side,
stirs me.

And I open my heart
to the soft blending
of your words,

from a thousand wings,
in your touch.

March

In the sequins dark,
warming heart of stones
open the tides
with shadows of whale bones
in the white orchards moonlight.

In the cold light
of early spring,
damp leaves coldly press the ground.
Winter's snow has vanished
and left its imprint on your side.

Your heart has opened
and the sun's hand passes over me.
Black boughs steam
in the new language of air
speaking as warm.

Gone now with your dark eyes—
only your kiss remains,

with the haunting west moon.

April

Rain and sun become music.

A Red-winged blackbird,
bobs on a blade of grass.

An eagle lifts a fish from the lake,
effortlessly.

And the grunions come home
with the tide.

And in the night's mouth,
the air leaves a warm, sleeping breath
around a yellow moon.

In the black pond's reflection,
peep frogs shout their desire.

Spring rain has thrown its nets,
earth inspires for tomorrow's cities,
of green and crimson.

Time returns,
into the body of another.

Like a bird flying through smoke,
and the sea falling into itself.

May

The air was on fire,
the heat soared all day—
extremely hot for May.

The afternoon sky turned black,
red eyes of a sunset
peeked through,
opening ribbons of light
down to the horizon.

A sea in the air—
rhythm of a sunset
that lifts across music and blood,
the smell of rose,
red over black.

It is the siren's song
that she sweetly sings,
for May flowers
on the sea of May.

White roses
in oceans field,
with winds, white music
spraying the air
with doves.

June

In the sky
lifting over fields of night
the white sand unfolded warm
across the vesper plain.

The white petals
of the moon
rippled on the pond.

On the shore, girls in white dresses
were dancing with flowers
and sprigs of jasmine.

And I tasted your lips
on a sweet tongue of air
in a laughing, silent breeze.

And your heart spoke to me
in the night,
on a sea blue path

lifting in the air
like a waltz,
sliding across the breath.

July

Across the summer's night,
the moon's longing
crept about in the darkness,
animal and heart.

Awakened
from the iris of the land,
the sea heated
out of a fragile glass,
breathed deeply
for a taste of air.

Even balanced,
surprised in the opening of her eyes,
the day leapt up warm out of her thighs.

Long-legged sky was waiting
and his loin was a hunting flame
and her heart without borders
loved it all.

August

The heat of the day
was the fire she left me with.

From the warm earth,
opaque, forgotten heart.

Soft echo,
golden body now awake.

She stood in the doorway crying,
more beautiful
then I could ever love her.

And she wore white linen
so I would always remember those days,
her red lips burning.

Sweet air washed summer,
her love in the marrow-shells
singing in the sand.

She vanished
with the sun setting
behind the hills,

a glimpse of her pink dress
left behind in the clouds.

September

Call up the autumn,
in its red
and deepening heart.

The leaves are turning to flowers.
Morning frost is on the window.
Trees are speaking louder
from earth, to heaven.

Now imminent,
the cold sea approaches,
its beard covers the willow's branch.

Birds tap the window sill,
to signal something is coming.

Yet you have not returned
from the last storm—
Not that I could have kept you
in summer.

Was it the fishers of the north wind
that caught you sleeping
or sea-bound thoughts
towards warmer islands?

I will find you again,
in the summer grass
staring up as before,
glowing in the light
of the moon.

October

October night,
hallow moon.

Black fingers in open sky
grabs the darkness across the mouth
burning voice of leaves.

Great river among the branches
rattle the swords awake.

Trees bow with lowered heads
and face the ancient wound—

Stare the giants hooded face
into the autumn wind,

cry roses heart of gold
as winter lifts its hand

and calls the girl across the field
to kiss her lips with snow.

November

November left blind
splendor in her voice,
calling out the frost
blankets of diamonds, speechless.

Hanging crystals branches
chimes broken bones
over the white earth, eyes gleaming.

In the sun
she cries the tears
that are not her own,
belonging to the child not yet born
beneath the earth singing.

In the air
the sweet, ageless tide
of fallen maples
and rotting oaks,
drift in and out over the snow.

Her face is of whispers that speak of death,
from the cold silence of the deer
in the deep woods there.

She enters through the doorway at dusk
and the heavy sky that she wears
falls away to smoke.

At the hearth
I feel the embers of her eyes,
as a spring of flames
crackle across my heart.

December

It is December
not even the moon can disguise her.

Cold, of the night,
sweet smelling musk.

Like the rose
opening the sun—
A breeze in the language of the night
speaks of the stones,
and the hearts
and the blood of each.

It is December
and the wings in my heart
one silent, one drawn out,
flutter within the roots
and the sky.

And the stars are shining,
a thousand voices
over the earth.

I remember other Decembers
and of a sadness I inherited,
that sings from within
searching for the fallen light.

ABOUT THE AUTHOR

Coy Williams was born in Waterford
Connecticut where he grew up with the
romance of the woods and the sea. He now
resides in Napa California. He holds a BA
degree in Art; MA in Creative writing. His
poems have appeared in, Pacific Sun Literary
review, Oasis, Bitterroot and The American-
Quarterly. Williams is the author of several
books of poetry, including his most recent,
Pearl Fishers and Wandering Girls Of Light